Elf Adventure

Journal

©2017 Elite Online Publishing
63 East 11400 South ☐Suite #230
Sandy, UT 84070
info@EliteOnlinePublishing.com

ALL RIGHTS RESERVED. This book contains material protected under International and Federal Copyright Laws and Treaties. Any unauthorized reprint or use of this material is prohibited. No part of this book may be reproduced or transmitted in any form or by any means electronic or mechanical including photocopying, recording, or by any information storage and retrieval system without express written permission from the author/publisher.

ISBN-13: 978-0-692-89706-5
ISBN-10: 0692897062

The Daily Adventures of your Elf   Date:_____

This Elf Journal Belongs to

Name

_____

Elf's Name

_____

Year

_____

The Daily Adventures of your Elf   Date:_____

The Daily Adventures of your Elf   Date:_____

The Daily Adventures of your Elf					Date:_____

Christmas Wish List:

_____

_____

_____

_____

_____

_____

_____

_____

_____

The Daily Adventures of your Elf   Date:_____

ABOUT MY ELF

My Elf's Birth Date: _____

My Elf's Country of Birth: _____

My Elf's eye color is: _____

My Elf's hair color is: _____

I think my Elf likes to eat: _____

I think my Elf likes to play: _____

I think my Elf's favorite color is: _____

My favorite things about my Elf is:_____

_____

_____

_____

The Daily Adventures of your Elf				Date:_____

Draw Your Elf

The Daily Adventures of your Elf   Date:_____

1. Where was your Elf when you woke up?

_____

_____

_____

_____

_____

Draw or place a photo or sticker here:

The Daily Adventures of your Elf   Date:_____

2. Last night the Elf...

_____

_____

_____

_____

_____

_____

<u>Draw or place a photo or Sticker here:</u>

The Daily Adventures of your Elf   Date:_____

3. What did the Elf do today?
_____

_____

_____

_____

_____

_____

Draw or place a photo or Sticker here:

The Daily Adventures of your Elf   Date:_____

4. Nice things the Elf will tell Santa I did today:

_____

_____

_____

_____

_____

Draw or place a photo or Sticker here:

The Daily Adventures of your Elf		Date:_____

1. Where was your Elf when you woke up?

_____

_____

_____

_____

_____

Draw or place a photo or sticker here:

The Daily Adventures of your Elf   Date:_____

2. Last night the Elf...

_____

_____

_____

_____

_____

_____

<u>Draw or place a photo or Sticker here:</u>

The Daily Adventures of your Elf   Date:_____

3. What did the Elf do today?

_____

_____

_____

_____

_____

_____

Draw or place a photo or Sticker here:

The Daily Adventures of your Elf					Date:_____

4. Nice things the Elf will tell Santa I did today:

_____

_____

_____

_____

_____

<u>Draw or place a photo or Sticker here:</u>

The Daily Adventures of your Elf   Date:_____

1. Where was your Elf when you woke up?

_____

_____

_____

_____

_____

Draw or place a photo or Sticker here:

The Daily Adventures of your Elf   Date:_____

2. Last night the Elf...

_____

_____

_____

_____

_____

_____

Draw or place a photo or Sticker here:

The Daily Adventures of your Elf   Date:_____

3. What did the Elf do today?
_____

_____

_____

_____

_____

_____

Draw or place a photo or Sticker here:

The Daily Adventures of your Elf   Date:_____

4. Nice things the Elf will tell Santa I did today:

_____

_____

_____

_____

_____

Draw or place a photo or Sticker here:

The Daily Adventures of your Elf   Date:_____

1. Where was your Elf when you woke up?

_____

_____

_____

_____

_____

Draw or place a photo or Sticker here:

The Daily Adventures of your Elf   Date:_____

2. Last night the Elf...

_____

_____

_____

_____

_____

_____

Draw or place a photo or sticker here:

The Daily Adventures of your Elf   Date:_____

3. What did the Elf do today?
_____

_____

_____

_____

_____

_____

Draw or place a photo or sticker here:

The Daily Adventures of your Elf   Date:_____

4. Nice things the Elf will tell Santa I did today:

_____

_____

_____

_____

_____

_____

<u>Draw or place a photo or Sticker here:</u>

The Daily Adventures of your Elf   Date:_____

1. Where was your Elf when you woke up?

_____

_____

_____

_____

_____

Draw or place a photo or sticker here:

The Daily Adventures of your Elf   Date:_____

2. Last night the Elf...

_____

_____

_____

_____

_____

_____

Draw or place a photo or Sticker here:

The Daily Adventures of your Elf   Date:_____

3. What did the Elf do today?

_____

_____

_____

_____

_____

_____

Draw or place a photo or Sticker here:

The Daily Adventures of your Elf   Date:_____

4. Nice things the Elf will tell Santa I did today:

_____

_____

_____

_____

_____

<u>Draw or place a photo or Sticker here:</u>

The Daily Adventures of your Elf   Date:_____

1. Where was your Elf when you woke up?

_____

_____

_____

_____

_____

Draw or place a photo or Sticker here:

The Daily Adventures of your Elf   Date:_____

2. Last night the Elf...

_____

_____

_____

_____

_____

_____

Draw or place a photo or Sticker here:

The Daily Adventures of your Elf   Date:_____

3. What did the Elf do today?
_____

_____

_____

_____

_____

_____

Draw or place a photo or sticker here:

The Daily Adventures of your Elf   Date:_____

4. Nice things the Elf will tell Santa I did today:

_____

_____

_____

_____

_____

_____

Draw or place a photo or Sticker here:

The Daily Adventures of your Elf   Date:_____

1. Where was your Elf when you woke up?

_____

_____

_____

_____

_____

Draw or place a photo or Sticker here:

The Daily Adventures of your Elf   Date:_____

2. Last night the Elf...

_____

_____

_____

_____

_____

Draw or place a photo or Sticker here:

The Daily Adventures of your Elf   Date:_____

3. What did the Elf do today?

_____

_____

_____

_____

_____

_____

Draw or place a photo or Sticker here:

Date:_____

4. Nice things the Elf will tell Santa I did today:

_____

_____

_____

_____

_____

<u>Draw or place a photo or Sticker here:</u>

The Daily Adventures of your Elf   Date:_____

1. Where was your Elf when you woke up?

_____

_____

_____

_____

_____

<u>Draw or place a photo or Sticker here:</u>

The Daily Adventures of your Elf   Date:_____

2. Last night the Elf...

_____

_____

_____

_____

_____

_____

_____

<u>Draw or place a photo or Sticker here:</u>

The Daily Adventures of your Elf   Date:_____

3. What did the Elf do today?

_____

_____

_____

_____

_____

_____

Draw or place a photo or sticker here:

The Daily Adventures of your Elf   Date:_____

4. Nice things the Elf will tell Santa I did today:

_____

_____

_____

_____

_____

Draw or place a photo or Sticker here:

The Daily Adventures of your Elf   Date:_____

1. Where was your Elf when you woke up?

_____

_____

_____

_____

_____

Draw or place a photo or Sticker here:

The Daily Adventures of your Elf   Date:_____

2. Last night the Elf...

_____

_____

_____

_____

_____

_____

Draw or place a photo or Sticker here:

The Daily Adventures of your Elf						Date:_____

3. What did the Elf do today?

_____

_____

_____

_____

_____

_____

Draw or place a photo or Sticker here:

4. Nice things the Elf will tell Santa I did today:

_____

_____

_____

_____

_____

_____

Draw or place a photo or sticker here:

1. Where was your Elf when you woke up?

_____

_____

_____

_____

_____

Draw or place a photo or sticker here:

Date:_____

2. Last night the Elf...

_____

_____

_____

_____

_____

Draw or place a photo or Sticker here:

The Daily Adventures of your Elf   Date:_____

3. What did the Elf do today?
_____

_____

_____

_____

_____

_____

Draw or place a photo or sticker here:

The Daily Adventures of your Elf　　　　　　　　　Date:_____

4. Nice things the Elf will tell Santa I did today:

_____

_____

_____

_____

_____

<u>Draw or place a photo or Sticker here:</u>

The Daily Adventures of your Elf   Date:_____

1. Where was your Elf when you woke up?

_____

_____

_____

_____

_____

Draw or place a photo or sticker here:

The Daily Adventures of your Elf Date:_____

2. Last night the Elf...

_____

_____

_____

_____

_____

_____

Draw or place a photo or sticker here:

The Daily Adventures of your Elf   Date:_____

3. What did the Elf do today?

_____

_____

_____

_____

_____

_____

Draw or place a photo or sticker here:

The Daily Adventures of your Elf   Date:_____

4. Nice things the Elf will tell Santa I did today:

_____

_____

_____

_____

_____

Draw or place a photo or Sticker here:

The Daily Adventures of your Elf   Date:_____

1. Where was your Elf when you woke up?

_____

_____

_____

_____

_____

Draw or place a photo or sticker here:

The Daily Adventures of your Elf   Date:_____

2. Last night the Elf...

_____

_____

_____

_____

_____

Draw or place a photo or Sticker here:

The Daily Adventures of your Elf　　　　　　　　　Date:_____

3. What did the Elf do today?

_____

_____

_____

_____

_____

_____

Draw or place a photo or Sticker here:

The Daily Adventures of your Elf   Date:_____

4. Nice things the Elf will tell Santa I did today:

_____

_____

_____

_____

_____

<u>Draw or place a photo or Sticker here:</u>

The Daily Adventures of your Elf   Date:_____

1. Where was your Elf when you woke up?

_____

_____

_____

_____

_____

Draw or place a photo or sticker here:

The Daily Adventures of your Elf   Date:_____

2. Last night the ELf...

_____

_____

_____

_____

_____

Draw or place a photo or Sticker here:

The Daily Adventures of your Elf   Date:_____

3. What did the Elf do today?
_____

_____

_____

_____

_____

_____

Draw or place a photo or Sticker here:

The Daily Adventures of your Elf   Date:_____

4. Nice things the Elf will tell Santa I did today:

_____

_____

_____

_____

_____

<u>Draw or place a photo or Sticker here:</u>

The Daily Adventures of your Elf   Date:_____

1. Where was your Elf when you woke up?

_____

_____

_____

_____

_____

Draw or place a photo or Sticker here:

The Daily Adventures of your Elf   Date:_____

2. Last night the Elf...

_____

_____

_____

_____

_____

<u>Draw or place a photo or Sticker here:</u>

The Daily Adventures of your Elf   Date:_____

3. What did the Elf do today?
_____

_____

_____

_____

_____

_____

Draw or place a photo or sticker here:

Date:_____

The Daily Adventures of your Elf

4. Nice things the Elf will tell Santa I did today:

_____

_____

_____

_____

_____

_____

Draw or place a photo or Sticker here:

The Daily Adventures of your Elf   Date:_____

1. Where was your Elf when you woke up?

_____

_____

_____

_____

_____

Draw or place a photo or Sticker here:

The Daily Adventures of your Elf   Date:_____

2. Last night the Elf...

_____

_____

_____

_____

_____

_____

Draw or place a photo or Sticker here:

The Daily Adventures of your Elf					Date:_____

3. What did the Elf do today?

_____

_____

_____

_____

_____

_____

Draw or place a photo or Sticker here:

The Daily Adventures of your Elf   Date:_____

4. Nice things the Elf will tell Santa I did today:

_____

_____

_____

_____

_____

<u>Draw or place a photo or Sticker here:</u>

The Daily Adventures of your Elf   Date:_____

1. Where was your Elf when you woke up?

_____

_____

_____

_____

_____

Draw or place a photo or sticker here:

The Daily Adventures of your Elf   Date:_____

2. Last night the Elf...

_____

_____

_____

_____

_____

_____

<u>Draw or place a photo or Sticker here:</u>

The Daily Adventures of your Elf   Date:_____

3. What did the Elf do today?
_____

_____

_____

_____

_____

_____

Draw or place a photo or sticker here:

The Daily Adventures of your Elf   Date:_____

4. Nice things the Elf will tell Santa I did today:

_____

_____

_____

_____

_____

_____

Draw or place a photo or Sticker here:

The Daily Adventures of your Elf   Date:_____

1. Where was your Elf when you woke up?

_____

_____

_____

_____

_____

Draw or place a photo or Sticker here:

The Daily Adventures of your Elf   Date:_____

2. Last night the Elf...

_____

_____

_____

_____

_____

Draw or place a photo or Sticker here:

The Daily Adventures of your Elf   Date:_____

3. What did the Elf do today?
_____

_____

_____

_____

_____

_____

Draw or place a photo or Sticker here:

The Daily Adventures of your Elf						Date:_____

4. Nice things the Elf will tell Santa I did today:

_____

_____

_____

_____

_____

_____

<u>Draw or place a photo or Sticker here:</u>

The Daily Adventures of your Elf   Date:_____

1. Where was your Elf when you woke up?

_____

_____

_____

_____

_____

Draw or place a photo or Sticker here:

The Daily Adventures of your Elf   Date:_____

2. Last night the Elf...

_____

_____

_____

_____

_____

_____

Draw or place a photo or Sticker here:

The Daily Adventures of your Elf   Date:_____

3. What did the Elf do today?

_____

_____

_____

_____

_____

_____

Draw or place a photo or Sticker here:

The Daily Adventures of your Elf   Date:_____

4. Nice things the Elf will tell Santa I did today:

_____

_____

_____

_____

_____

_____

Draw or place a photo or sticker here:

The Daily Adventures of your Elf   Date:_____

1. Where was your Elf when you woke up?

_____

_____

_____

_____

_____

Draw or place a photo or sticker here:

The Daily Adventures of your Elf   Date:_____

2. Last night the Elf...

_____

_____

_____

_____

_____

_____

Draw or place a photo or Sticker here:

The Daily Adventures of your Elf   Date:_____

3. What did the Elf do today?

_____

_____

_____

_____

_____

_____

<u>Draw or place a photo or sticker here:</u>

The Daily Adventures of your Elf   Date:_____

4. Nice things the Elf will tell Santa I did today:

_____

_____

_____

_____

_____

<u>Draw or place a photo or Sticker here:</u>

The Daily Adventures of your Elf Date:_____

1. Where was your Elf when you woke up?

_____

_____

_____

_____

_____

<u>Draw or place a photo or Sticker here:</u>

The Daily Adventures of your Elf   Date:_____

2. Last night the Elf...

_____

_____

_____

_____

_____

Draw or place a photo or sticker here:

The Daily Adventures of your Elf					Date:_____

3. What did the Elf do today?
_____

_____

_____

_____

_____

_____

Draw or place a photo or Sticker here:

The Daily Adventures of your Elf   Date:_____

4. Nice things the Elf will tell Santa I did today:

_____

_____

_____

_____

_____

_____

<u>Draw or place a photo or Sticker here:</u>

The Daily Adventures of your Elf   Date:_____

The Daily Adventures of your Elf   Date:_____

1. Where was your Elf when you woke up?

_____

_____

_____

_____

_____

<u>Draw or place a photo or Sticker here:</u>

The Daily Adventures of your Elf   Date:_____

2. Last night the Elf...

_____

_____

_____

_____

_____

_____

Draw or place a photo or Sticker here:

The Daily Adventures of your Elf   Date:_____

3. What did the Elf do today?

_____

_____

_____

_____

_____

_____

<u>Draw or place a photo or Sticker here:</u>

The Daily Adventures of your Elf   Date:_____

4. Nice things the Elf will tell Santa I did today:

_____

_____

_____

_____

_____

Draw or place a photo or Sticker here:

The Daily Adventures of your Elf   Date:_____

1. Where was your Elf when you woke up?

_____

_____

_____

_____

_____

Draw or place a photo or Sticker here:

The Daily Adventures of your Elf   Date:_____

2. Last night the Elf...

_____

_____

_____

_____

_____

<u>Draw or place a photo or Sticker here:</u>

The Daily Adventures of your Elf   Date:_____

3. What did the Elf do today?

_____

_____

_____

_____

_____

_____

Draw or place a photo or sticker here:

The Daily Adventures of your Elf   Date:_____

4. Nice things the Elf will tell Santa I did today:

_____

_____

_____

_____

_____

Draw or place a photo or Sticker here:

The Daily Adventures of your Elf   Date:_____

1. Where was your Elf when you woke up?

_____

_____

_____

_____

_____

Draw or place a photo or sticker here:

The Daily Adventures of your Elf   Date:_____

2. Last night the Elf...

_____

_____

_____

_____

_____

_____

<u>Draw or place a photo or Sticker here:</u>

The Daily Adventures of your Elf   Date:_____

3. What did the Elf do today?
_____

_____

_____

_____

_____

_____

Draw or place a photo or Sticker here:

The Daily Adventures of your Elf	Date:_____

4. Nice things the Elf will tell Santa I did today:

_____

_____

_____

_____

_____

_____

<u>Draw or place a photo or Sticker here:</u>

The Daily Adventures of your Elf   Date:_____

1. Where was your Elf when you woke up?

_____

_____

_____

_____

_____

Draw or place a photo or Sticker here:

The Daily Adventures of your Elf   Date:_____

2. Last night the Elf...

_____

_____

_____

_____

_____

_____

Draw or place a photo or Sticker here:

The Daily Adventures of your Elf   Date:_____

3. What did the Elf do today?

_____

_____

_____

_____

_____

_____

Draw or place a photo or Sticker here:

The Daily Adventures of your Elf   Date:_____

4. Nice things the Elf will tell Santa I did today:

_____

_____

_____

_____

_____

<u>Draw or place a photo or Sticker here:</u>

The Daily Adventures of your Elf   Date:_____

1. Where was your Elf when you woke up?

_____

_____

_____

_____

_____

Draw or place a photo or Sticker here:

2. Last night the Elf...

_____

_____

_____

_____

_____

_____

<u>Draw or place a photo or Sticker here:</u>

The Daily Adventures of your Elf　　　　　　　　　　Date:_____

3. What did the Elf do today?

_____

_____

_____

_____

_____

_____

Draw or place a photo or Sticker here:

The Daily Adventures of your Elf   Date:_____

4. Nice things the Elf will tell Santa I did today:

_____

_____

_____

_____

_____

Draw or place a photo or Sticker here:

The Daily Adventures of your Elf   Date:_____

From Your Elf,

Golly gee, can you believe it? Tomorrow is Christmas!! But, that means it's time for me to go back to the North Pole to tell Santa how you behaved these past few weeks. I hope you enjoy playing with all the presents Santa's going to give you. I'll miss you very much, and I had so much fun being with you. I loved playing hide-and-seek with you. You're such a good finder! I hope you continue to be good everyday, and I can't wait to play with you again next year.

Off to the North Pole I go! I'll tell Santa you said hi!!

Love,

Your Elf

Date:_____

The Daily Adventures of your Elf

write and Draw

Write and Draw

The Daily Adventures of your Elf   Date:_____

Write and Draw

The Daily Adventures of your Elf   Date:_____

Write and Draw

Write and Draw

Write and Draw

The Daily Adventures of your Elf	Date:_____

write and Draw

The Daily Adventures of your Elf Date:_____

Write and Draw

The Daily Adventures of your Elf   Date:_____

Write and Draw

Write and Draw

The Daily Adventures of your Elf

Date:_____

write and Draw

The Daily Adventures of your Elf   Date:_____

Write and Draw

The Daily Adventures of your Elf   Date:_____

write and Draw

The Daily Adventures of your Elf   Date:_____

write and Draw

write and Draw

The Daily Adventures of your Elf   Date:_____

Write and Draw

Write and Draw

Write and Draw

The Daily Adventures of your Elf   Date:_____

Write and Draw

Write and Draw

Write and Draw

The Daily Adventures of your Elf   Date:_____

write and Draw

Date:_____

Write and Draw

The Daily Adventures of your Elf   Date:_____

Write and Draw

Elf Certificate

Hurray! You have filled up your

Elf Adventure Book

with a lot of fun drawings and Memories

Go to www.eliteonlinepublishing.com/elf_certificate

And get your Official Certificate from the

North Pole.

Once you get your certificate your Elf will send you private messages throughout the year.

Do you Draw?

If you would like **your drawing** of an Elf to be on one of our **Elf Adventure Book Covers,** submit it to the website below.

You will have Your name and age displayed on the cover of the Elf Adventure book as the cover designer.

All you need to do is:
1. Scan and submit Your Drawing as 300 dpi, 8.5 x 11 size to our Website: http://eliteonlinepublishing.com/shelf-elf-journal/

or mail it to:

      Elf Adventure
      63 East 11400 South #230
      Sandy, Utah 84070

2. Childs' name and age.
3. Date of drawing.
4. Contact information.

Elite Online Publishing helps busy entrepreneurs, business leaders, and professional athletes create, publish, and market their book to build their business and brand. Elite is passionate about authors sharing their stories, knowledge and expertise to help others. **Owners**, Melanie Johnson & Jenn Foster, have published many authors on Amazon, iTunes, Nook, Google Books and more. All of the Elite Online Publishing Authors have become #1 best sellers! Listen to the Hot Chicks Write Hot Books Podcast that is featured on iTunes and Stitcher Radio. You can also watch or listen to the Video Podcast, Elite Expert Insider. Jenn & Melanie interview authors and business experts about their road to success. They talk about their books and the book writing process. To learn more visit: **www.EliteOnlinePublishing.com** or call 1(832) 572-5285

How to Write and Capture Your Family Yearbook

A Story Starter Guide & Workbook to Write Your Family's Stories, Memories & Activities of the Calendar Year (Elite Story Starters Series) Available on Amazon Now. http://amzn.to/2hPeX91

www.ingramcontent.com/pod-product-compliance
Lightning Source LLC
Chambersburg PA
CBHW060533010526
44107CB00059B/2629